Fruit Infused Water

50 QUICK & EASY RECIPES
FOR DELICIOUS & HEALTHY HYDRATION

ELLE GARNER

http://ElleGarner.com
http://MyTakePress.com

Published by: **My Take Press**

More Books by Elle Garner:

Permanent Weight Loss: Choose Thin!

Drink Pure Water

Contents

Introduction

I'm an author, optimist, health enthusiast, wife, mom, and dog lover. I love to write, read, travel, go to the ocean, spend time with family, play with my Goldendoodle, hike, sail, and am passionate about all things green and organic.

I'm not a snob about my preference for organic food, and I realize everyone doesn't think like I do, or live like I do - and that is perfectly okay.

With all of that said, there are some "truths" that are universal and important to health.

Drinking water every day is necessary for energy, detoxification, healthy weight, and LIFE.

I'll take it one step further and say that drinking PURE water is vitally important. I wrote a book on this topic (Drink Pure Water: Pure Water and Hydration are Critical for Performance, Weight Loss, and Health. Learn Why and Where to Find it, Make it and Get it) so I won't belabor that point here. But it is an important one!

One of the common complaints I get from readers of my first two books is that they hate drinking water. Some of them can barely get one or two glasses down per day.

I typically enjoy a glass of cold, pure water, but in order to drink the recommended amount of water per day (and I usually try to drink more than that), I've found that fruit-infused waters make a huge difference in the amount of water I drink daily.

I also find that psychologically I look forward to water that is slightly flavored with some of my favorite fruits and herbs – and that is much better for you than dreading every sip you take.

I truly believe that the way we feel about our water, the food we eat, and everything we put into our body impacts what is does when it gets there. That's why the principles in Permanent Weight Loss: Choose Thin! Worked for me, and are working for many others. Diets don't work when you hate what you are putting into your mouth. In order for permanent weight loss to truly work, you have to like and enjoy the foods you eat. The same applies to drinking water.

This is how **Fruit Infused Water: 50 Quick & Easy Recipes For Delicious & Healthy Hydration** came into being.

Drinking pure water, and enjoying it, is a critical component of everything I write about, live, and teach. It's my hope that this book will enable you to being enjoying pure, healthy water with your favorite fruits and herbs, in copious amounts, on a *daily* basis.

Just in case you are wondering, commercial juices and even commercially bottled flavored waters often have unhealthy ingredients and preservatives. Read the labels! It's our position that plastic is unhealthy to drink from. Period.

You can say goodbye to sodas, sugary fruit juices, and commercially bottled flavored waters with these healthy, refreshing, hydrating, truly natural, quick and easy fruit infused water recipes.

You *can* truly hydrate your body with pure (or filtered) water infused with delicious and fresh fruits, herbs, and vegetables. I use **organic** for ALL my fruit, herb, and vegetable waters, but in the end that is a personal preference.

How much water should you drink? It differs to some degree for each person, and you should absolutely consult your personal medical doctor or health care provider before following any of the recipes in this book. You and your doctor know best. One rule of thumb is to drink half of your body weight in ounces of water. Another is to drink six to eight glasses (8 oz) of water each day. These are minimums for most people, but again you may have a medical condition that preempts the average recommendations. Talk to your doctor!

PLEASE NOTE: This is not medical advice, nor am I a medical professional. Every person and body is different so PLEASE consult with your medical doctor or health care provider before consuming the fruit infused water recipes in this book. Only you and your doctor know if you have a medical condition that prohibits fruits or drinking water as recommended here. If you do, please discuss with your health care provider if these recipes can be modified safely for you.

** IF you take **prescription drugs**, please check with your doctor or pharmacist **BEFORE** consuming fruit infused waters. Some drugs (not all) do not interact well with certain fruits.

Warmly,
Elle

What Are Fruit Infused Waters?

Fruit infused waters are exactly that – water that has been infused with fruit. Most of the recipes in this book are fruit infused, however, you'll find some that include small amounts of herbs (like mint), and even vegetables.

This is a very simple approach to flavoring water, and it will not taste overly sweet or sugary. If that is what you are looking for – you won't find it here. My goal is to help you begin to truly enjoy simple, pure, delicious, and healthy flavors in an effort to help you drink more water.

You can literally use almost any kind of fruit that you enjoy in flavoring your water.

We take our favorite fruit, cut it into pieces or slices, add it to a pitcher of water and let it set for 2-12 hours.

Here are some Basic Rules and Tips:

- It's best to only keep the fruit in the water for approximately 24 hours (That's my personal preference). Any more than that and some fruits can begin to go bad. I make an exception to this when using fresh lemons in flavoring water, yet I never go beyond leaving fruit in refrigerated water for more than 48 hours.
- Use glass jars, pitchers, or just about any glass container.
- Always refrigerate the water and fruit.
- Refrigerate minimally for 2 hours before drinking, and some fruits require several hours before you begin to taste the infused flavors.
- It is always best to use pure, filtered water.
- Some fruit (like strawberries) will flavor the water best when sliced.
- ALWAYS wash the fruit thoroughly before adding to the water.
- Triple the recipe when you have company in a larger glass container (with a pouring spout if possible) and add ice. It will keep for hours and is easy for guests to refill, as they are thirsty.

Fresh vs. Frozen: Always use fresh fruit whenever possible; in season is best. When fruit is out of season, organic, frozen fruit is a great alternative.

Fresh Herbs: You can use whatever herbs you happen to have on hand. I always have mint in my garden or refrigerator, but it is fun to experiment with lavender, rosemary, basil, sage, etc.

Quantities: Use any size jar or glass container that you happen to have on hand. I picked up some thin glass pitchers at Target because our refrigerator always seems to be packed. You can adjust these recipes based on the size of your container; most recipes here are perfect in a 2-quart container.

Honestly, it's not possible to add too much fruit, yet we've experimented with each of these recipes to add just the right amount of fruit to create the flavor we want, without adding too much, and thereby wasting fruit that can otherwise be eaten.

We will also talk about the known health benefits of each of the fruit and herb referenced in our recipes. If there's something in particular you know your body needs, you'll be able to identify the fruits that can help you add that to your diet quickly and easily.

This is not rocket science. All the recipes in this book are relatively quick, easy, and simple -- because the more complicated they are the less likely you are to actually make them consistently.

It's my goal to help you get into the habit of making fruit infused water *daily*, and hopefully begin on a journey to keeping your body well hydrated, every single day.

Take note of how you feel, because a well-hydrated body provides more energy, vitality, and a better sense of well-being. Most people don't know what it feels like to be properly hydrated, and that is a fact.

It's my goal to help you create simple, delicious, and easy fruit infused waters that will encourage you to drink more pure, healthy water.

So, let's get started!

List Of What You Need

- BPA free containers, preferably glass. Glass doesn't absorb any flavors of previous liquids, and it's safer and healthier in my opinion, to use glass rather than worry whether or not a plastic container has BPA in it or not.
- A knife. A small pairing knife for smaller fruit, and a longer knife for watermelon-sized fruit is adequate. Keep them sharp and in good condition to truly make this quick and easy, and prevent injury.
- Pure water. This can be from your home if you have clean well water, from a tested deep-earth spring, or from purified water. Some people prefer their own tap water, and if you are okay with that it will work perfectly fine. I prefer purified water, but in the end it is important for all of us to hydrate well throughout the day, so if that means you need to use tap water, than use it.
- A wooden or stainless spoon. This is not a requirement, but there are times that I use the handle of a wooden spoon to stir the fruit if I have more than one kind in the glass pitcher. I also use it to gently smash/bruise the herbs. This helps to release their oil and flavor into the water; and should be done just prior to adding them to the water. I usually "muddle" or bruise berries just ever so slightly, as well, in order to bring more flavor into the infusion.
- Your chosen fruit(s) and herb(s). Make sure you wash all ingredients thoroughly before cutting. You can also use a very small amount of vinegar in the water if your fruit is not organic, or simply to make sure many, if not all contaminants are removed.

- Ice. Again, not a requirement, but if you like your water extra cold, or if you are keeping it out of the refrigerator, add ice.

Simple, quick, easy, and you likely already have everything in your home that you need to begin making delicious and healthy fruit infused waters.

Recipes are listed in order of my personal preference, beginning with the most simple, one ingredient fruit infused waters, to the more complex toward the end of the book.

We resisted "naming" our waters based on ingredients in the interest of keeping this quick and easy for you to find a recipe that contains the ingredients you already have in your refrigerator, or a recipe that can meet your cravings! I find it frustrating to have to search through recipes to find one that I can easily and quickly make with ingredients I currently have on had – that won't happen with this book. All recipes are named with the ingredients they contain for your convenience.

We want to keep this simple and doable for you. Once it becomes a habit, most people enjoy experimenting with waters that may take more than a few minutes to prepare.

List of Fruits and Herbs

Here's a complete list of the best fruits to use in fruit infused water. Most but not all are used in the recipes contained in this book. We also use some vegetables and herbs. Those are listed below, as well. You do not need to purchase all of these, and hopefully you already have some in your home. Purchase what you need based on how often you visit the farmer's market or supermarket near you.

Fresh is always best, and the most nutritious, so purchase only what you need for the water and for your own personal food consumption.

You don't have to use organic, but I highly recommend it.

ORGANIC FRUITS:

Strawberries
Blueberries
Blackberries
Raspberries
Oranges
Watermelon
Lemon
Lime
Papaya
Apple
Cherries
Mango
Nectarine

Peach
Pear
Pineapple
Grapefruit
Kiwi
Cranberry
Pomegranate
Tangerine
Cantaloupe
Honeydew melon
Cucumber
Coconut
Ginger

ORGANIC HERBS:

Mint
Rosemary
Lavender
Sage
Basil
Thyme
Cinnamon
Vanilla

OPTIONAL INGREDIENTS:

Coconut water
Stevia

**Add a very small amount of Stevia if you want to add a slight bit of sweetness to your water. We recommend that you begin simply with the fruit and allow your taste buds to begin to adjust to the simple pleasures these waters can bring.

I'm providing some of these ingredients simply to provide you with options. If quick and easy is truly what you are looking for, the one and two ingredient fruit infused water recipes will suffice. Keep it simple!

If you want something a little more complicated for entertaining or a celebration, we've provided recipes for that, too. Fruit colors are beautiful, and they make are impressive when served. Check the Table of Contents, and you can jump to those recipes immediately.

ONE INGREDIENT FRUIT INFUSED WATERS

Each of these recipes contains just one fruit, making them very quick and easy to make.

Some require the time to slice the fruit, but if that is too much for you, go with one of the berry recipes that requires no slicing and in few hours you will have a delicious, hydrating, fruit infused water to enjoy!

Plan ahead by making them right before you go to bed and they are ready by morning. Alternatively, make it before you go to work or school and you will have delicious, healthy water ready for you when you arrive home.

We provide an estimate of how long each type of fruit takes to infuse the water within each recipe.

If all you need is just a slight flavor to make water palatable to you, you will love what you find inside these pages!

For those who want a stronger flavor, follow the steps recommended above and you will always have a delicious, flavorful, and healthy fruit infused water available.

If the flavor isn't strong enough for you, slice the fruit or berries before adding even if the recipe doesn't call for that. In the end, this is about creating delicious and healthy waters that you WANT to drink.

Lemon Infused Water

This is the ultimate in simple, quick, and easy. It is the perfect drink first thing in the morning, with lunch and dinner, and even right before bed. Basically, this is one of our favorites.

Lemon Benefits:

- Alkaline to the body
- High in Vitamin C
- Contain 22 anti-cancer compounds
- Powerful antibacterial properties
- Cleansing and detoxifying
- Aids digestion

Combine:

2 Quarts pure Water
1 lemon, thinly sliced (remove seeds)
Ice (if desired)

Let it sit for 1 hour minimally before drinking. If you are short on time, simply squeeze a small amount of the lemon into the water and then add the rest of the slices. Drink immediately!

Strawberry Infused Water

Our second favorite, strawberry water is one of the most flavorful, and like lemons, the water takes on the flavor of the fruit quickly.

Strawberry Benefits:

- High in antioxidants
- Anti-inflammatory
- Rich in B-complex
- Contain potassium, magnesium, and Vitamin K – all important for bone health
- Anti-aging properties
- High in Vitamin C

Combine:

2 quarts pure water
1-2 cups, sliced strawberries
Ice (if desired)

The water will take on the flavor of sweet strawberries very quickly (usually within 1-2 hours), and is refreshing. If you like or feel the need for sweet, this is one of the simplest and most healthy ways to get it.

Raspberry Infused Water

Raspberries are my favorite fruit, but because the water takes a bit longer to take on the raspberry flavor, this is number three on the list.

Raspberry Benefits:

- High in antioxidants
- High in folate, magnesium, and other vitamins and minerals
- Anti-inflammatory
- Diet-friendly
- Anti-aging
- High in Vitamin C

Combine:

2 quarts pure water
¾-1 cup of raspberries
Ice (if desired)

After 2-3 hours you will just begin to taste the essence of raspberry in the water. We recommend leaving this in the refrigerator overnight, cut the raspberries in half, or making it first thing in the morning to enjoy when you come home from school or work. This is extremely light and refreshing, especially in a tall glass of ice.

Blackberry Infused Water

Blackberry's can be a bit more stubborn in sharing their flavor. We find that cutting just a few in half, or adding significantly more of them makes a big difference in delivering delicious, blackberry flavor-full water.

Blackberry Benefits:

- Rich in bioflavonoids and Vitamin C
- One of the highest antioxidant levels of all fruits
- Anti-aging
- Prolonged consumption helps keep your brain alert
- Anti-inflammatory

Combine:

2 quarts pure water
2 cups of blackberries (slice a few to help infuse flavor more
    quickly)
Ice (if desired)

Like raspberries, blackberries take a while before they begin to flavor the water. Leave them overnight, slice them, or make this in the morning before heading off to work or school. It will be perfect by the time you get home.

Blueberry Infused Water

Blueberries are similar to blackberries in that they take quite a while before their flavor truly infuses water. You can add herbs (like mint) to help this along, or cut a few of the blueberries when adding them to the water.

Blueberry Benefits:

- Highest level of antioxidants of any other fresh fruit or vegetable
- Preserve vision
- Banish belly fat (the polyphenos in blueberries also reduce risk for metabolic syndrome)
- High in manganese (important for bone development)
- Excellent for memory, brain, and heart health
- Anti-cancer benefits

Combine:

2 quarts pure water
2 cups of blueberries (some sliced to enhance flavor)
Ice (if desired)

If you are not a big fan of blueberries, add mint, or some blackberries or raspberries (or all three) to the water. Blueberries (organic) are a powerhouse of health. Don't miss this one!

Orange Infused Water

This is another fruit infused water that will take on the flavor of the fruit almost immediately! If you love oranges, this will be right up your alley. It is very sweet, and doesn't take a lot of fruit to infuse the water quickly.

Orange Benefits:
- Vitamin C (They are known for it! – 1 orange contains nearly 100% of the RDA of vitamin C.)
- 170 different phytonutrients and more than 60 flavonoids in one orange
- Good for the brain (high in folate)
- Strengthen the immune system
- Anti-inflammatory
- Rich in calcium (good for teeth and bone health)

Combine:

1 quarts pure water
1 orange, sliced (think or thick – your choice)
Ice (if desired)

Orange-infused water is sweet, delicious, healthy, and refreshing. Who needs commercial orange juice? Try this yummy alternative, and if you keep the water for just 24 hours you can eat the oranges rather than discard them.

Watermelon Infused Water

Watermelon water? Isn't watermelon mostly water? Yes, it is – and it makes a delicious, light fruit infused water!

Watermelon Benefits:

- High in antioxidants
- Improves heart health – high in lycopene
- Eye health - High in beta carotene
- High in vitamin C
- High in amino acids

Combine:

1 quarts pure water
1-2 cups of watermelon, cubed (remove seeds)
Ice (if desired)

Watermelon will flavor-infuse the water quickly, so if you need a fast, refreshing drink for company, this one fits the bill. Add some mint or even a small squeeze of lime.

Lime Infused Water

Lime infused water is one of my favorites. When we go to a restaurant, I always order lime with my water and almost every time I get lemon. Why is that? For a special treat when eating out, I ask for bottled sparkling water with a splash of cranberry and lime; delicious and far more healthy that most of the alternatives!

Lime Benefits:

- High in vitamin C
- High in calcium and folate
- High in antioxidants
- Weight Loss benefits
- Anti-inflammatory
- Aids Digestion

Combine:

2 quarts pure water
1 lime, sliced
Ice (recommended)

** Many of my friends add a small amount of stevia to their lime water. I love the flavor of lime, but if you don't, this is a great option.

Grapefruit Infused Water

Grapefruit is another one of my favorite fruits. I know, you've heard this a few times at this point, but given the option I could live on fruit and be perfectly happy! When I was pregnant with my son, I craved Grapefruit. Later I found out that that it contained many of the nutrients he needed during that phase of development. To this day, I still eat copious amounts of grapefruit, and it is one of my favorite essential oils; something about it just makes me feel happy.

Grapefruit Benefits:

- Loaded with Vitamin C
- High in Vitamin A, Potassium, Folate, B5, & Lycopene
- Contains salicylic acid (reported to help break down inorganic calcium in the body that can build up and aggravate arthritis symptoms)
- Good for skin
- Anti-aging

Combine:

2 quarts pure water
½ grapefruit, thinly sliced

Note that grapefruit is one of the fruits I used in the book cover. I think it's a gorgeous fruit.

Cucumber Infused Water

You often see cucumber water in spas, and you'll see why when you read the benefits below. This is a simple, very light, healthy, and refreshing water to enjoy any time of the day. Cucumbers have a very subtle and light flavor, so give this several hours to infuse prior to drinking.

Cucumber Benefits:

- Aids digestion and weight loss
- Excellent for detox
- High in B vitamins (great mid-day pick up!)
- Anti-cancer
- Good for skin and hair
- Promotes joint health

Combine:

2 quarts pure water
1/4 to 3/4 cucumber, sliced (depending on the size of the cucumber)
Ice (if desired)

The peeling of the cucumber is very good for you, so be sure to include it. Buy organic, if possible, as they are often sprayed with pesticides.

Vanilla Infused Water

Vanilla is used in cooking, aromatherapy, and now fruit infused waters. (: It has a gentle, calming aroma, and researchers are finding that there are many potential health benefits.

Vanilla Benefits:

- Antimicrobial
- Possible aphrodisiac
- Anti-carcinogen (Current research is exploring vanillin's properties and abilities to inhibit chromosome breakage and other promising benefits.)
- Vitamins and trace minerals

Combine:

2 Quarts pure water
1-2 vanilla beans

** This will need to infuse for at least 8-10 hours.

~~~~~

This will conclude our single ingredient waters, although you can certainly take any of the fruit in the list at the beginning of this book by itself to make delicious fruit infused water.

Find the fruits you love best, and experiment with them to find the amount that adds just the right amount of flavor for you. What's perfect for me may be too little for you, and visa versa.

Next we'll move on to combinations of fruits and/or fruits and herbs for slightly more sophisticated fruit waters and flavor.

~~~~~

TWO INGREDIENT FRUIT INFUSED WATERS

All the recipes below contain two ingredients, but don't hesitate to add another if you find yourself inspired by some of your favorite fruits and herbs. In some cases, simply adding a few springs of mint, rosemary, or lavender can create just the right blend of flavors.

Experiment and have fun! Or if you are short on time, simply make one of the tested twenty two-ingredient recipes we've included in this section. You, your family, and your friends will love them!

By now you know that I always focus on organic fruits and herbs. I truly believe they are more nutritious and healthy for you. If you don't typically buy organic, try them and see if you notice a difference.

Raspberry and Lime Infused Water

You already know the benefits of these fruits if you have read through the One Ingredient section. From this point on we will only mention the benefits of newly referenced ingredients. There's no point in repeating information; this is all about quick and easy.

Combine:

> 2 Quarts pure water
> ½ - ¾ cup of raspberries
> ½ lime, sliced
> Ice (if desired)

Fresh and sassy, raspberry and lime create a delicious and lively blend of flavor.

Grapefruit and Lime Infused Water

Combine:

2 Quarts pure water
½ Grapefruit (adjust depending on desired flavor strength)
½ Lime
Ice (if desired)

There's a nice zing in this fruit infused water, in addition to lots of Vitamin C, and other nutrients that are very good for you. This drink is one of my favorite afternoon pick-me-ups.

Lemon and Blueberry Infused Water

Combine:

2 Quarts pure water
½ Lemon
½ to ¾ cup of blueberries
Ice (if desired)

This combination reminds me a bit of blueberry pie. It makes my mouth salivate just thinking about it! It's a powerful and healthy pair, and perfect on a summer day -- or any day for that matter.

Cucumber and Mint Infused Water

Combine:

> 2 Quarts pure water
> ½ cucumber, sliced
> 3-5 sprigs of Mint (gently pounded with a wooden spoon)
> Ice (if desired)

Delicious on a warm summer day, this combination is very light and refreshing. It pairs perfectly with almost any meal, or can be enjoyed by itself. This is a big favorite at weddings, spas, and resorts.

Lemon and Lime Infused Water

Combine:

2 Quarts pure water
½ lemon, sliced
½ lime, sliced
Ice (if desired)

You don't have to choose between lemons or limes – enjoy them both together! Together they are packed with good-for-you nutrients, and the perfect morning or pick-me-up refresher. (The color combination is also nice if you are entertaining.)

Cucumber and Lemon Infused Water

Combine:

2 quarts pure water
½ cucumber, sliced
½ lemon, sliced
Ice (if desired)

This drink is beautiful, especially if you slice both fruits very thin. It's light, refreshing, healthy, thirst quenching, and rejuvenating.

Cinnamon and Apple Infused Water

Apple Benefits:

- Nutrition (You know the old adage, "an apple a day", well there's a good reason for it!)
- Weight Loss – researchers believe the antioxidants & pectin contribute to this.
- May protect against Metabolic Syndrome

Cinnamon Benefits:

- Possible blood sugar control benefits
- Anti-microbial
- Antioxidant
- May aid in weight loss

Combine:

2 quarts pure water
½ - ¾ apple, sliced (more if you prefer)
2 cinnamon sticks

This is a sweet and spicy water that is perfect on a cool day. Apples are packed with nutrition. Give this infusion plenty of time to mature – it will be worth it!

Strawberry and Lemon Infused Water

Combine:

2 quarts pure water
1 cup strawberries, sliced
½ lemon, sliced
Ice (if desired)

Does this make your mouth water? We think it is a perfect and beautiful summer drink combination. It's sweet (without being too sweet), refreshing, and light, with just the right amount of zing from the lemon. It's sure to be a hit with guests; and don't save it just for summer. If you live in a cold weather area, and can get organic strawberries in the winter, this is the perfect reminder of summer.

Strawberry and Vanilla Infused Water

Combine:

>2 quarts pure water
>1 cup+ strawberries, sliced
>1-2 organic vanilla beans
>Ice (recommended)

Let this infuse for several hours. The gentle taste of vanilla combined with sweet strawberries creates yummy, refreshing, and gentle-flavored water. It's decadent.

Lime and Honeydew Melon Infused Water

Honeydew benefits:

- Packed with Vitamin C
- Good source of Potassium
- Good source of B vitamins
- Good source of trace minerals

Combine:

2 Quarts pure water
½ Lime
1 cup honeydew melon, cubed
Ice (if desired)

Honeydew is naturally sweet and gentle-flavored, add this to lime and you have a delicious, refreshing, healthful, and gentle summer drink.

Watermelon and Cantaloupe Infused Water

Combine:

2 Quarts pure water
1 cup watermelon, cubed
1 cup cantaloupe, cubed
Ice (recommended)

These melons compliment each other well and create a light, refreshing summer drink. Enjoy with ice. Mint and Rosemary both work well, if you want to add an herb.

Basil and Raspberry Infused Water

Basil Benefits:

- Anti-inflammatory properties
- Powerful antioxidants
- Promotes healthy skin
- Good for digestion

Combine:

2 quarts pure water
2-4 basil leaves, gently pounded
½ to ¾ cup of raspberries
Ice (if desired)

To be perfectly honest, I was skeptical about this combination until I tried it. I adjusted my friend's recipe to suit my taste (slightly less basil), but I definitely enjoy the combination. If you like basil, try it with other fruits, as well.

Lemon and Ginger Infused Water

Ginger Benefits:

- Aids digestion
- Aids absorption & assimilation of nutrients
- Reduces gas & flatulence
- Anti-inflammatory properties
- May help rid the body of congestion

Combine:

2 quarts pure water
½ Lemon
3 cubes or slices of ginger (adjust as preferred)
Ice (recommended)

** Add mint if desired

This drink is wonderful all year round! Lemon and ginger are a wonderful combination, and we've intentionally kept this light. I've tried recipes that recommend larger quantities, but since this is all about quick and easy this is the recipe that I find works best; but don't hesitate to adjust if you LOVE ginger.

Lime and Papaya Infused Water

Papaya Benefits:

- Good source of Vitamin A and C
- Rich source of phyto-nutrients
- Good source of B vitamins
- Shown to be anti-inflammatory and anti-parasitic

Combine:

2 quarts pure water
½ lime, sliced
1 cup papaya, cubed
Ice (if desired)

Papaya is sweet and delicious all by itself, add lime, and you have a delicious and healthy combination that is great for digestion, cool, and refreshing.

Mango and Pineapple Infused Water

Mango Benefits:

- Compounds in Mango fruit have been found to protect against some cancers
- Eye Health
- Skin Health
- Alkaline enhancing
- Improves digestion

Pineapple Benefits:

- Anti-inflammatory
- Improves digestion
- High in antioxidants
- High in Vitamins A, C and E

Combine:

2 quarts pure water
¾ cup pineapple, sliced or cubed
¾ cup mango, cubed
Ice (recommended)

Let this infuse for at least a few hours prior to drinking, and you will almost feel like you are in the tropics! Both fruits are naturally sweet, healthy, and delicious. This is a great combination.

Cantaloupe and Mint Fruit Water

Cantaloupe Benefits:

- Excellent source of Vitamin C and A
- Good source of B Vitamins
- Antioxidant
- Anti-inflammatory support

Combine:

2 quarts pure water
3-6 mint sprigs (gently pound with wooden spoon)
1 cup cantaloupe, cubed
Ice (recommended)

Light, refreshing, and low in calories, this drink is delicious on a warm day, or perfect in the afternoon. If you are a fan of cantaloupe, this variation might be just right for you.

Orange and Lemon Fruit Water

Combine:

2 quarts pure water
½ to 1 full Orange, sliced
½ lemon, sliced
Ice (if desired)

Where do we start? This is delicious! Orange is naturally sweet and combined with lemon this is a scrumptious, healthy, and satisfying drink. Perfect for a hot summer day, or any time of year.

Blueberries and Apple Fruit Water

Combine:

 2 quarts pure water
 1 cup blueberries
 ½ to 1 apple, sliced (remove seeds)

POWERFUL and healthy drink that tastes as great as it looks beautiful. Give this plenty of time to infuse, as the blueberries take longer because of their skin. You can also cut a few of the blueberries to give it a head start.

Cherries and Vanilla Fruit Water

Cherry Benefits:

- Anti-inflammatory
- High in flavonoids (powerful antioxidants that help fight free radicals)
- Contain melatonin and may help you sleep
- Good source of potassium
- High in B Vitamins

Combine:

2 quarts pure water
1 cup of cherries, sliced in half & pitted
1-3 vanilla beans
Ice (if desired)

Decadent *and* healthy is a great way to describe this fruit infused water. This drink tastes great all day long, and can easily be enjoyed before bed with no worry that it will disrupt sleep. Studies have shown that even 2 Tablespoons of tart cherry juice prior to bed can be as effective as a melatonin supplement (USDA).

This is the last two-ingredient recipe, but you can literally combine any of your favorite fruits (although we do not recommend bananas in water) to create a delicious, healthy, hydrating fruit infused water.

Blackberry and Sage Infused Water

Combine:

2 quarts pure water
1 cup blackberries, muddle or slice a few
2 sage leaves
Ice (if desired)

This infused water has a mild, refreshing flavor. The sage calms slightly tart blackberries down (depending on how fresh and in-season the berries are), and it's a wonderful combination. If you have both ingredients on hand, give this a try!

THREE INGREDIENT FRUIT INFUSED WATERS

Although a bit more complex, you can still make these waters easily and quickly.

Go straight for the berry recipes if you are short on time and big on flavor. If you have an extra two to five minutes, we have some delicious 3-ingredient recipes that will be huge hits with family and friends.

Fruit infused waters have become a way of life in our home, and my refrigerator is rarely without them. I hope this book will inspire you to drink more pure water, and help you become more aware of the difference in how your body feels (and performs) when it is well-hydrated.

Grapefruit, Orange, and Lemon Fruit Water

Combine:

 2 quarts pure water
 ½ grapefruit, sliced
 ½ orange, sliced
 ½ lemon, sliced
 Ice (as desired)

Slice the fruit very thin, and the water will look simply beautiful! Try these flavors together before you judge the combination because it is delicious. You can change the amount of fruit used, just keep the quantity consistent between the grapefruit and orange. ½ lemon tends to be enough in 2 quarts of water. You can begin drinking this water within an hour after infusion begins.

Cinnamon, Apple, and Ginger Infused Water

Combine:

2 quarts pure water
2 cinnamon sticks
1 apple, sliced (remove seeds)
Ginger, 2-3 fresh slices or cubes
Ice (if desired)

This is a more robust and spicy combination. If you love the 'taste of fall' or have an upset stomach, this may be just what the doctor ordered. Adjust the cinnamon and ginger based on your desired level of spice.

Lemon, Basil, and Blueberry Infused Water

Combine:

2 quarts pure water
½ Lemon
2-3 basil leaves (gently pound with wooden spoon)
¾ cup of blueberries
Ice (if desired)

A delicious and energizing combination, lemon, basil, and blueberry pack a powerful digestive and healthful infusion.

Strawberry, Mint, and Lemon Infused Water

Combine:

> 2 quarts pure water
> ¾ cup of strawberries, sliced
> 3-5 sprigs of mint (pound gently with wooden spoon)
> ½ lemon, sliced
> Ice (if desired)

Light, sweet, and refreshing, this combination is beautiful in a pitcher or a glass liquid dispenser with a spout for a party.

Orange, Pineapple, and Strawberry Fruit Water

Combine:

2 quarts pure water
½ Orange, slicked
1 Cup Strawberries, sliced
1 Cup Pineapple, cubed or sliced

This combination creates a lightly sweet fruit water with a tropical flare. It is a refreshing and very flavorful water; packed with Vitamin C.

Blueberry, Strawberry and Mint Infused Water

Combine:

2 quarts pure water
1 cup strawberries, sliced
3-5 mint sprigs (gently pound with wooden spoon)
¾ cup blueberries
Ice (if desired)

Perfect for summer holidays, or just about any day, this fruit and herb infused mix is light, fresh, sweet, and satisfying; not to mention filled with healthful ingredients.

Strawberry, Raspberry, and Blueberry Fruit Water

Combine:

2 quarts pure water
½ cup strawberries, sliced
½ to ¾ o ¾ cup of raspberries
½ cup of blueberries (slice a few for enhanced flavor)
Ice (if desired)

The strawberries have a tendency to overpower the other berries in this mix. Combine just enough to create the blend you like, and slice a few of the raspberries and blueberries to enhance their flavor into the infusion. This is one of my favorites of the three ingredient fruit infused waters.

Strawberries, Blueberries, and Vanilla Infused Water

Combine:

    2 quarts pure water
    ½ cup strawberries, sliced
    ¾ cup blueberries
    1-2 vanilla beans

Vanilla adds a sweet twist to this infusion. Use it sparingly, and pair it only with lighter foods because of the more intense flavor. Give this infusion several hours before drinking.

Kiwi, Pineapple, Lemon Fruit Infusion

Kiwi Benefits:

- High in phytonutrients
- High in folic acid
- Good source of Vitamin C, and 10% of the RDA of Vitamin E
- Good source of trace minerals

Combine:

2 quarts pure water
1 kiwi, sliced
1 cup of pineapple, sliced or cubed
½ lemon, sliced
Ice (if desired)

Kiwi is another favorite fruit, and when combined with pineapple and lemon, it creates a light, sweet, highly-refreshing and delicious fruit infused water. We love this especially in the summer – or even in the winter when we *wish* we were in the tropics. (:

Tangerine, Mint, and Cantaloupe Infused Water

Tangerine Benefits:

- Loaded with flavonoids (anticancer properties/neutralize free radicals)
- High in Vitamin C and Vitamin A
- Good source of folate
- Good source of potassium

Combine:

2 quarts pure water
1 tangerine, sliced (remove seeds)
2-5 mint sprigs, lightly pounded with a wooden spoon
1 cup cantaloupe, cubed
Ice (if desired)

Fun, sweet, refreshing, and healthy, this fruit infused water is beautiful, delicious, refreshing, and perfect on a warm summer day.

Blueberry, Apple, and Mint Infused Water

Combine:

2 quarts pure water
½ - ¾ cup of blueberries
½ apple, sliced thin
2-5 Mint sprigs, lightly pounded with a wooden spoon

This infusion has a very light flavor – just enough to add dimension and interest. Apples and blueberries are a nice pair (even in pies!) and the mint adds just enough difference to make this threesome delicious.

Cucumber, Watermelon, and Cantaloupe Fruit Water

Combine

2 quarts pure water
½ cucumber, sliced thin
1 cup watermelon, cubed
1 cup cantaloupe, cubed
Ice (if desired

These melons all have a very light and sweet flavor. Combined – they are melon heaven. The flavors should infuse within approximately 2 hours, and I keep this in the refrigerator only for 24 hours before discarding. Apart from the more simple fruit infusions, it's tough to beat this for a light, refreshing, delicious fruit water drink.

FOUR INGREDIENT FRUIT INFUSED WATERS

These infusions take a little bit more prep time, but not significantly so. They create delicious flavor combinations and look simply beautiful. They are perfect for entertaining, but you don't have to entertain to enjoy them. I've seen them served at weddings, resorts, spas, and in my home.

The bottom line? ENJOY them. Drink them. Feel the *difference* healthy hydration makes in your body.

Raspberry, Blackberry, Blueberry, and Mint

Combine:

2 quarts pure water
½ cup raspberries
½ cup blackberries
½ cup blueberries
3-5 Mint sprigs, lightly pounded with a wooden spoon

These dark berries are packed with flavor and nutrition. Mint adds just the right hint of herb, and they require at least 4 hours before you begin to taste the infusion. It is best to let them infuse for 4-6 hours or longer before drinking.

Pineapple, Orange, Mint and Ginger

Combine:

2 quarts pure water
1 cup pineapple, cubed
1 orange, sliced (seeds removed)
3-5 mint springs, lightly pounded with a wooden spoon
2-3 slices or cubes of ginger (adjust per your preference)

Delicious and incredibly satisfying infusion of sweet fruits and healthy herbs, with ginger adding a powerful flavor punch. It's a bit of a tropical and Asian blend that is very refreshing.

Blueberry, Raspberry, Vanilla, and Rosemary

Rosemary Benefits:

- Improved brain performance (Northumbria University, U.K.)
- Anti-inflammatory
- Anti-aging
- High in iron, calcium, and Vitamin B6

Combine:

2 quarts pure water
½ cup blueberries
½ cup raspberries
2 vanilla beans
Several sprigs of rosemary (approx. 1 teaspoon)

This infused water has almost exotic flavor; rich, refreshing, sweet, and herbal. Experiment with the rosemary to attain the balance you prefer. I usually add slightly less than 1 teaspoon to a 2-quart infusion.

Lemon (or Lime), Blueberry, Blackberry, and Raspberry

Combine:

2 quarts pure water
½ Lemon (or Lime), sliced
¼ cup Blueberries
¼ cup Blackberries
¼ cup Raspberries
Ice (if desired)

Slice a few if not all of the berries to enhance the infusion flavor. Let this infuse for at least 3 hours before drinking. This is slightly tart combined with sweet (depending on the ripeness of your berries), and incredibly delicious with ice. You and your guests will love it.

Lemon, Strawberry, Blueberry, and Raspberry

Combine:

2 quarts pure water
½ lemon, sliced
½ cup strawberries, sliced
½ cup blueberries
½ cup raspberries
Ice (if desired)

Slice a few of the blueberries and raspberries to enhance the infusion's berry flavor, and help them catch up with the lemon and strawberry. Let this infuse for at least three hours to allow for the flavors to blend. Drink over ice, and enjoy this delicious, fresh, and hydrating beverage.

FIVE INGREDIENT FRUIT, SPICE, AND HERB INFUSIONS

Kick it up a notch with our five ingredient infusions!

Many of these include a spice or herb to add a new dimension to these light and refreshing waters. Enjoy them all year around -- by yourself, and with your friends and family. They are sure to be a hit, and maybe just maybe you will encourage your friends and family to begin truly hydrating their bodies with delicious, natural, and hydrating infused waters.

Watermelon, Strawberry, Raspberry, Lemon, and Mint

Combine:

2 quarts pure water
½ cup watermelon, cubed
½ cup strawberries, sliced
½ cup raspberries
½ lemon, sliced
5 mint leaves (lightly pounded with a wooden spoon)
Ice (as desired)

This is one of our favorite 5-ingredient infusions! This combination is red-heavy; yet light, sweet, and just a perfectly yummy blend of fruits and herbs. It's also incredibly beautiful and perfect when you're entertaining. Put a few pitchers on the table and watch your guests "oooo" and "ahhh".

Blueberry, Strawberry, Raspberry, Blackberry, and Mint

Combine:

2 quarts pure water
1/4 cup blueberries
1/4 cup strawberries, sliced
1/4 cup raspberries
1/4 cup blackberries
Ice (if desired)

Doesn't this sound delicious? You will want to slice a few of each of the berries to help infuse flavor more quickly. We personally reduce the amount of each type of berry to avoid "overcrowding" but if you want your infusion to be heavy on flavor, you can add up to ½ cup of each of the berries listed above, as desired.

Give this infusion 3 hours and then enjoy!

Raspberry, Blueberry, Strawberry, Blackberry, and Cinnamon

Combine:

> 2 quarts pure water
> ¼ cup raspberries
> ¼ cup blueberries
> ¼ cup strawberries, sliced
> ¼ cup blackberries
> 1 stick cinnamon
> Ice (if desired)

This infusion is light, with a slight kick of cinnamon. As you read earlier, cinnamon has a number of benefits, and many believe it helps deter appetite – but you do not need to be dieting to enjoy this one! It's decadent, rich yet light, and delicious.

As mentioned in the above recipes, slice some of these berries in order to truly benefit from the infused flavors. Give this at least 2 hours to infuse prior to drinking.

Blueberry, Papaya, Strawberry, Lemon, and Cinnamon

Combine:

2 quarts pure water
¼ cup blueberries
¼ cup papaya, cubed
¼ cup strawberries, sliced
½ lemon, sliced
1 stick cinnamon
Ice (recommended)

The papaya in this recipe adds powerful nutrients and antioxidants in addition to a nice tropical flavor enhanced by the cinnamon. You will want to slick some of these blueberries in order to give them a chance to compete with these other flavors. Combined they are scrumptious. We love this iced during the summer!

Apple, Strawberry, Raspberry, Blueberry, and Cinnamon

Combine:

2 quarts pure water
½ apple, sliced
¼ cup strawberries, sliced
¼ cup raspberries
¼ cup blueberries
1 stick cinnamon
Ice (recommended)

Although we have not used apple often in these recipes, this is one infusion you will not want to miss, and you don't have to wait until fall *unless* you want the freshest apples possible.

Give this infusion 3 hours before drinking, and slice some of the berries in order to balance the flavors. We prefer it with ice, but this is delicious even at room temperature.

The combinations are nearly limitless when it comes to fruit, herb, spice, and even vegetable infusions! The recipes contained in this book are recipes that are tested and proven in my kitchen, with family and friends.

It's my hope that you will enjoy them as much (or more) as we do, and that you will quickly realize the mental and physical difference it makes when you hydrate adequately with pure water.

Experiment with new combinations and if you find one that you like, please stop by my website or Facebook page to let us know!

Website: ElleGarner.com

Facebook: http://www.facebook.com/ElleGarnerWriter

Please remember to check with your doctor before trying any of these recipes, especially if you take prescription drugs, or have any type of health issue. Heck, even if you don't it just makes sense to touch base with your doctor or health care provider. You can recommend this book to them while you're at it. (-:

Fruit Infused Water is also available in paperback at http://ElleGarner.com/paperback.

About Elle

Elle Garner is an author, optimist, health enthusiast, wife, mom, and dog lover. She uses her love for writing and health as a catalyst to write about topics she's passionate about.

Elle loves to write, read, travel, go to the ocean, spend time with family, play with her dog, hike, boating, and all things green and organic. She also loves NFL Football and the New England Patriots. (GO Patriots!)

She believes achieving health, vibrant energy, a positive life and a successful life is easier than you think, and it's her mission in life to make a difference for as many people as she can.

She also loves connecting with her readers!

Website: ElleGarner.com
Facebook https://www.facebook.com/ElleGarnerWriter
Amazon Author page: https://www.Twitter.com/Elle_Garner

Elle's Books:

Permanent Weight Loss Choose thin: ElleGarner.com/thin

Drink Pure Water: ElleGarner.com/water

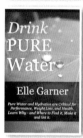

Fruit Infused Water: ElleGarner.com/fruit

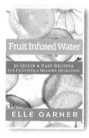

Other Books You May Like:

Wheat Belly
Eat Real Essentials
Juicing for Beginners

Sign up for New Release notification at
ElleGarner.com. When you do, you'll get a
BONUS PDF with additional photos and recipes!

Please share this book with your friends, because
they need to hydrate and be healthy, too.

28994847R00049

Made in the USA
Lexington, KY
09 January 2014